You Matter

'52 Achievable Self-Care Choices"

By Lisa Desgagne

YOU MATTER

ISBN-13: 978-1530387595
ISBN-10: 1530387590

ILLUSTRATIONS BY: AMBER SOLBERG

Dedication

This book is dedicated to my husband Paul and my children; Stefan, Danielle and Joshua, who have always believed in me even during the moments that I did not believe in myself.

Acknowledgements

First, I would like to thank my husband Paul Desgagne, without his belief in me, none of this would have been possible. His generous and constant support and enthusiasm is what encourages me to always realize that I am truly capable of doing anything I set my mind to.

My second big thank you goes to my children; Stefan, Danielle and Joshua, who have grown into such loving, amazing and responsible young adults which has now allowed me the opportunity to step into the next exciting chapter of my life.

Finally, I would like to thank my Business Coach and mentor Jan Eden, for her never ending brilliant, creative ideas and her constant support and encouragement.

Give Yourself Permission

One of the key elements in making self-care a priority is giving yourself permission to do what feels good for you not what you think you should do. Allow yourself to take a few minutes each day to nurture the parts of yourself that need nurturing knowing that by doing so you will be able to serve others in a more calm and effective way.

You Matter

*"26 Achievable **No Cost** Self-Care Choices"*

Working Out

Making time to exercise is the No.1 most important highly recommended no cost self-care activity in keeping a healthy body and mind.

Indulge in a Leisurely Bath

Taking a long, well-deserved hot bath or shower is a welcomed indulgence especially after a strenuous workout or chaotic day.

Giving Thanks

Upon waking or before falling asleep, take time every day to say "Thank You" to the Universe for giving you another day filled with blessings to enjoy.

Lounge in Bed

Stay in bed for an extra 10 or 20 minutes and read the daily news. Discovering what is happening in the world reminds us to never take life for granted.

Cherish Down Time

Remember to take time out of your busy day to make time to meditate, reflect, read or lie still for several minutes and be one with the day.

Create a Sacred Space

Create a sacred space to retreat to that offers peace and serenity. You deserve it.

Read

Indulging in a good book temporarily transcends ones mind.

Colouring and Doodling

This childlike creative exercise can open your mind to finding solutions to problems you may otherwise never discover.

Spending Time Outside in Nature

Being one with nature will instantly clear the mental noise and chaos that gets trapped in our brains.

Commune with Nature

Planting your bare feet firmly on grass or dirt instantly connects you to feeling the natural healing of mother earth's energy coming up through your feet into your legs and the rest of your body.

Keep Your Daily Routine Simple and Organized

Being consistently organized will bring calm and peace into your life.

Spend Precious Time With Friends

Laugh until your stomach hurts. Magic happens when spending time sharing and reminiscing with close friends.

Just Breathe

Stop what you are doing and take just two or three deep breaths and then continue on with whatever it was you were doing.

Giving Back

Brighten someone's day. Random acts of kindness can be visible or anony-mous. Making this a daily habit will fill your heart with joy and also brighten your day.

Turn Off the Noise

Eliminate any unnecessary noise pollution. Silence is calming and therapeutic.

Spend Time with Your Favourite People

Hanging out with your grown-up kids is like visiting the best parts of yourself.

Enjoy Favourite Things

Sometimes the smallest pleasures will bring huge amounts of joy and contentment.

Smile at Strangers

As people pass you by, make eye contact and say hello with a smile.

SING

Sing out loud, sing strong, sing in the shower. Just sing.

Dance

Dance like no one is watching.

Journal

Keep a journal close by and regularly capture your thoughts. Documenting these things puts you into a state of mindfulness that helps you gain perspective.

Cry When you Need to

Grab a box of tissue and enjoy a good cry. Shedding a few tears is mentally cleansing, releases toxins and shifts perception.

Go for a walk

Walking 20 minutes each day will rejuvenate your mind, comfort your soul and provide important physical health benefits.

Stop and Smell the Roses

Literally stop and smell a fragrant flower. It will immediately calm and transcend your mind.

Celebrate...

the simple pleasures of life or a big personal accomplishment that brings joy to your heart. Dance around the room or call a friend to share in your good news.

You Matter

"26 Daily 'At a Cost' Self-Care Choices"

Treat Yourself

You are worth it. Buy those new shoes, that favourite designer handbag, golf putter or something you have been longing for.

Invest in Yourself

Take the course that will educate or inspire you into becoming personally or professionally greater. Or hire a business/life coach who will help to propel you forward to the next level. The results received will be worth every penny.

Splurge on Expensive Bedding

Crawling into clean, luxurious and scrumptious bedding, at the end of a busy day, has a way of immediately releasing tension and stress.

Join a Gym

Get into shape and build new friendships while working out at a gym.

Engage a Personal Trainer

Hire a trainer to keep you accountable in achieving your fitness goals can be extremely rewarding.

Take Yourself on a Date

Go to a movie and dine alone before or after at your favourite restaurant. Having the confidence to sit by yourself in a public place is very liberating.

Organized Space

Working or living in a cluttered environment results in having a cluttered mind. If the task of organizing is too daunting hire a professional organizer to organize your home or office space. You will immediately see and feel the results.

Playing with Electronic Gadgets

Through intuitive play learning how electronics work can be mentally invigorating and enlightening.

Experience a Great Haircut

Pay extra for top hair stylist talent. Both men and women feel great after leaving with their hair falling perfectly into place.

Be with Yourself

Book a retreat to get to know yourself again. Take time to reflect on your goals and rekindle lost dreams.

Share a Mini Vacation with a Special Friend

Invite a friend to go off on a spa or golf weekend together. A change of scenery with a special friend can reenergize your spirit.

Enroll in Art or Music Lessons

Let your creative juices flow with the encouragement of an instructor who can help you bring out your inner "Picasso" or "Mozart".

Join an Adult Dance Class

Creatively moving your body in a structured adult dance class releases stress while opening up your brain to learn new dance combinations.

Enjoy a Sex Weekend Away with your Significant Other

Schedule time away and mark the dates in your calendar. The benefits of regular sex have been medically proven to reduce stress, lower blood pressure which will help you to live longer. You will comeback glowing and the benefits will last for weeks.

Make Regular Spa Appointments

Treat yourself to a pedicure, body treatment or facial. The calming atmosphere that a quality spa offers give you short reprieve from your hectic daily routine.

Retain Professional Help

Hire a counsellor, therapist or spiritual advisor when life becomes overwhelming. It is sometimes easier to talk to someone who doesn't know you to help you gain new perspective and insight.

Commit to Having Regular Massages

Massage is a healing discipline that reduces stress and pain. Significant physiological and psychological changes occur from the healing touch of regular massage.

Go to the Theatre

Support local talent by purchasing season tickets to a theater in your area. No need to travel to Broadway, some of the best talent is often right in our own neighbourhoods.

Visit an Art Gallery

Strolling through an art gallery can be extremely calming and relaxing. Invest in a piece of art that speaks to your soul and put it in a place where you can look at it everyday.

Do Something New, Exciting and Fun

To push you out of your comfort zone while at the same time conquering some underlying fears.

Take a Family Vacation

The money spent is an investment that will bond the family for a lifetime with laughter and timeless memories shared.

Hire a Housecleaner

There is no better experience after a busy day than coming home to a sparkling clean house.

Savour a Good Bottle of Wine

Periodically spurge on a really good bottle of wine. While you are sipping savour every decadent moment.

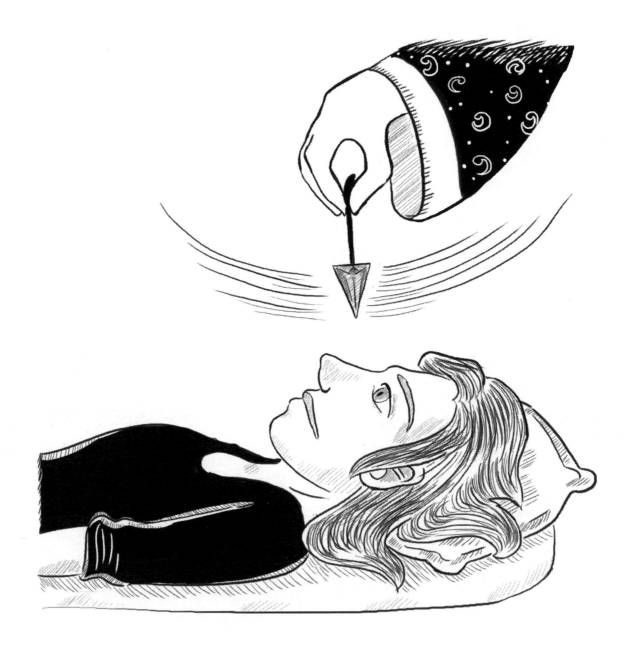

Book Regular Energy Healing Sessions

Find an energy healer whose discipline aligns with you and your values. Energy healing reduces stress and promotes relaxation. It also triggers the body's natural ability to heal and improve overall health and well-being.

Indulge in a Favourite Hobby

Give yourself a gift and invest in something that you love to do in your spare time that brings you joy and fulfillment.

Celebrate...

the simple pleasures of life or a big personal accomplishment with people you love.

Meet the Author

Lisa Desgagne was born in Alberta, Canada and has built her career as a Personal Growth Expert specializing in Self-Care, Life Transitions and how to conquer Self Limiting Fears. As an entrepreneurial wife, mother of three children, step-mother, grandmother, daughter, sister, friend, confidant and business owner, Lisa has dedicated her life to helping herself and others learn how to overcome enormous and eventful life changes and challenges.

What others say and know about Lisa

Lisa has insightful questions and fully listens to my answers with a calm, compassionate and accepting demeanor which leaves me feeling stronger and more emotionally equipped to deal with my life challenges.

-Holly

Lisa is always available and reliable for a quick chat or long conversation and her clear unbiased insights allow me to gain new perspectives.

-Christina

Lisa's innate ability to discern life's gifts and challenges so clearly is just one of her many strengths. My good fortune in knowing Lisa has enriched my life enormously and words simply cannot describe the level with which I cherish her and her wisdom.

-Laureen

Lisa's remarkable family values remind me, frequently, of recognizing my own values.

-Jennifer

41790297R10067

Made in the USA
Middletown, DE
23 March 2017